While You're Waiting for the Food to Come

While You're Waiting for the Food to Come

A Tabletop Science Activity Book

Experiments and tricks that can be done at
a restaurant, the dining room table,
or wherever food is served

by Eric Muller
illustrated by Eldon Doty

Orchard Books   New York

To Kay,
Where do you want to have dinner?
    —E.M.

Adults should supervise the participation of children
in the activities in this book whenever it is age or
otherwise appropriate to do so.

Text copyright © 1999 by Eric Muller
Illustrations copyright © 1999 by Eldon Doty
Originally copyrighted 1995 (copyright code Txu 679-361)

Orchard Books, A Grolier Company
95 Madison Avenue, New York, NY 10016

Manufactured in the United States of America
Printed and bound by Haddon Craftsmen
Book design by Mina Greenstein
The text of this book is set in 11 point Sabon.
The illustrations are created in Adobe Photoshop and Freehand.
10 9 8 7 6 5 4 3 2

Library of Congress Cataloging-in-Publication Data
Muller, Eric P.
While you're waiting for the food to come : a tabletop science activity book :
experiments and tricks that can be done at a restaurant or wherever food is
served / by Eric Muller; illustrated by Eldon Doty.
    p. cm. Includes bibliographical references.
Summary: A collection of science experiments and activities that can be done
where food is served, exploring such topics as the senses, gravity, and water.
ISBN 0-531-30199-0 (trade : alk. paper)
ISBN 0-531-07144-8 (pbk. : alk. paper)
1. Science—Experiments—Juvenile literature. [1. Science—Experiments.
2. Experiments.] I. Doty, Eldon, ill. II. Title.
Q164.M84   1999   507'.8—dc21   99-17168

PREFACE

After teaching science in public schools for many years in California, I took a year-long job on the East Coast to develop science curriculum. I loaded up my pickup and drove alone across the United States. The radio was broken, the air conditioner didn't work, and the springs in my seat were shot—all making for a very uncomfortable ride. By the time I hit the Great Plains, I took any opportunity to get out of my car, and found I was spending more and more time at roadside restaurants. While I sat there, waiting for the food to come, I played, experimented, and did tricks with anything and everything at the table.

As I passed through each state, I increased my repertoire and took notes on the activities I did. Fellow travelers, parents, kids, waiters, waitresses, and buspeople would come over to find out what I was doing and would often join me in my experiments. Not only was I having fun and meeting interesting people, but I was teaching science at the same time. I could have stayed at some restaurants for hours showing people activities, but I had to move on.

From road trip to publication, the activities presented here have been tested at hundreds of restaurants, dozens of classrooms, and numerous homes. I'd like to thank everybody who contributed to the creation of this volume. I tried to include as many people as I could in the acknowledgments.

I had a blast researching and writing *While You're Waiting for the Food to Come*. I hope you enjoy reading and doing the activities just as much.

Feed your body! Feed your mind!

CONTENTS

APPETIZERS
Activities to whet your appetite • 1

• • • • • • • • • • • • • • • • •

MAIN COURSES
Activities to sink your teeth into • 13

• • • • • • • • • • • • • • • • •

"I wonder what I'll have"—Doing science • 14

DESSERTS
Topping off your meal • 77

INTRODUCTION

Do you ever go to restaurants and just wait for the food to come? While you're waiting, do you get listless, restless, fidgety, fiddlesome, or just plain bored out of your gourd? Look around your table. What do you see? Do you just see a place to eat? A place to drink? A place to get bored out of your gourd? Or do you see a place to learn, experiment, and have fun? Well, with a little bit of imagination, ingenuity, and this handy-dandy guide, you can have a lot of food-time fun and learn something too (no, they are not mutually exclusive), all within the walls of a restaurant. This book can also provide hours of fun in a kitchen, at a picnic table, or on a beach blanket.

Your table can be more than just a place to put your food. It can be a place where you can challenge yourself and others. It can be a laboratory where you can perform scientific experiments. You can do science with almost everything on your table. Do you have a straw? A can of soda? Some ketchup? If you do, you could be on the road to learning about how an airplane flies or how the solar system is structured.

Since this is a restaurant science book, I've organized it like a menu. You may start out with an **Appetizer** or skip directly to a **Main Course**. An Appetizer is a hands-on activity to start you thinking and give you a taste of what you might find in other chapters of this book. Each chapter in the Main Courses section is packed full of rich, high-calorie activities that follow a specific scientific concept. If you read the introduction to each chapter, then you'll get a taste of what it contains.

As you'll soon find out, each chapter includes four to seven activities. Each activity has various symbols and is divided into sections. Dining alone or with a friend? To find out how many people are needed for each activity, check out the "people" indicator at the top of each activity. Do you have what it takes to make your experiment happen? Locate the list of

Ingredients to see what kind of materials you'll need. How is each experiment done? The **Recipe** section, along with the *Tips du Jour,* lists the steps, instructions, and hints to follow in order for you to get the most out of your science (and dining) experience. After you do an experiment, you should read the section called **Food for Thought**. Here you'll find an explanation of the scientific principles behind the activity you just completed. The section called **More to Chew On** links your tabletop activity with other events and phenomena. Several activities also contain a **Side Dish**. Side Dishes aren't just coleslaw or potato salad; they are suggestions for other experiments you can try.

So, while you're waiting for the food to come, try out a few of these activities and enjoy your dining and learning experience.

P.S. Some experiments require more preparation than others. So you might want to skim through this book before heading out to your chosen restaurant. Also, please remember to check with a parent first to make sure your chosen mealtime activity is appropriate. (The attention-attraction factor key at the top of each activity, described below, might help you determine this.) And be sure to leave a big tip for your server if an experiment goes awry!

ATTENTION-ATTRACTION FACTOR KEY
1. People at other tables probably won't notice what you're doing
2. People at other tables may notice what you're doing
3. Your table might get a lot of attention

1   2   3

Your seat is ready.
Please follow me.

APPETIZERS

Activities to whet your appetite

If you don't know where to start in this book, might I recommend an appetizer?

Each activity in this chapter is a tasty morsel that will introduce you to some basic concepts and leave you wanting more. If you're still hungry, turn to the chapter mentioned at the end of each appetizer. There is one appetizer for each chapter in the Main Courses section of this book. There you will find more mouthwatering tricks and delicious experiments to satisfy your appetite.

Bon appétit!

one person

FOLDS

Here's a question for you: How many times can you fold a piece of paper in half?

Have the people at your table guess a number and see who is right.

Ingredients

Paper place mat or paper napkin

Recipe

1 • Lay your place mat or napkin completely open and flat on a table.

2 • Fold the place mat or napkin in half. Continue to fold it in half as many times as you can. You might struggle with the last fold or two.

Food for Thought

How many times were you able to fold the place mat or napkin in half? Once? Twice? Two hundred? I bet you couldn't fold it more than eight times. That is probably a little less than you guessed.

A flat, open place mat (zero folds) has a paper thickness of only one layer. After one fold, you have two layers. After two folds, you have four layers; three folds, eight layers; and so on. Do you see a pattern here? Every time you fold the paper in half, you double the number of layers of paper. The more layers of paper, the thicker the bundle you have to fold and the harder it is to make the next fold. It gets really hard to fold 128 layers of paper and even harder to fold 256 layers of paper, which is how many layers of paper you have by your eighth fold.

2

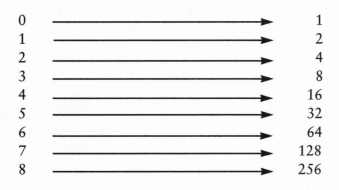

Number of folds		Layers
0	———————————▶	1
1	———————————▶	2
2	———————————▶	4
3	———————————▶	8
4	———————————▶	16
5	———————————▶	32
6	———————————▶	64
7	———————————▶	128
8	———————————▶	256

What numbers do you think would come next?

More to Chew On

If you investigated this paper puzzle and tried answering the question "How many times can you fold a piece of paper in half?," then you just did a true science experiment and you are a true scientist. This experiment might not win you the Nobel Prize (the highest honor in science), but it's a start. If you are curious, you have the single most important characteristic of a scientist. Turn to the chapter "I Wonder What I'll Have," on page 14, and find out more about doing science.

Have you ever had handmade Chinese noodles? They're really good. Have you ever seen someone make Chinese noodles? They're made by folding! One thick piece of noodle dough is folded in half again and again. Each time, the number of noodles doubles, and each time the noodles become thinner and thinner. After just a few folds, what was once a wad of dough becomes hundreds of delicate strands of noodles. Now that's Chow Fun!

IN BAD TASTE

**There is more flavor information in food than meets the tongue!
You can fool a friend's sense of taste with this one.**

Ingredients

Salad bar with lots of different types of food

Recipe

*Tip du Jour: You can also try this experiment with
different types of juices and soda pop.*

1 • Load your plate with foods that feel as if they have similar textures.
Check out the following for ideas and examples:

> apples and pears
> lemons and oranges
> carrots and radishes
> avocados and bananas
> potatoes and beets
> ~~mashed potatoes and applesauce~~
> olives and grapes
> different types of Jell-O or pudding

2 • Choose one person to be the taster and one person to be the server.
3 • The taster pinches his nose shut, opens his mouth, and closes his eyes.
4 • The server places a piece of food in the taster's mouth.
5 • The taster chews the food and moves it around in his mouth for a few
seconds.

6 • Before the taster swallows, ask him
what's in his mouth. Is he right or
wrong?
7 • Tell the taster to let go of his nose.
Does he change his guess?
8 • Switch jobs and try it again.

Don't you think it's weird that you couldn't tell the difference between different types of food with just the information from your tongue? When you make a decision or arrive at a conclusion, you want to have as much information as you can get. To help tell the difference between foods, you need the help of your nose.

Have you ever gotten a cold and a clogged nose? Food just doesn't taste as good, does it? That's because flavor information can't reach the odor receptors in your nose. Our noses can tell the difference between many different things, but our tongues can only detect a few flavors: bitter, sour, salty, and sweet. Most food flavor comes from our sense of smell, not our sense of taste. Only about 10 to 20 percent of flavor information comes from our tongue.

Besides bitter, sour, salty, and sweet, there is an additional flavor that scientists recently discovered we can taste—monosodium glutamate, or MSG. It has a meatlike flavor.

Besides taste and smell, there are three other ways of getting information inside our bodies: sight, hearing, and touch. These five ways are called our senses. Once information is inside our bodies, we handle it in various ways. To learn more about how we process information, turn to "What Goes In," starting on page 26.

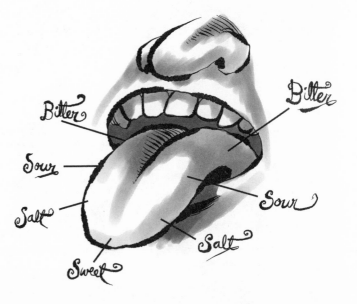

one person

CONDIMENT DIVER

**Make a delicious device that works like a submarine.
No, not the sandwich, the ship!**

Ingredients

Condiment packet: ketchup, soy sauce,
  hot sauce, or
  barbecue sauce
Clear plastic bottle
  (any size will do)
Tall glass of water

Recipe

*Tip du Jour: Many types of liquid condiment packets work.
Experiment and see which sauces work best.*

1 • First, you have to figure out which condiment packet
   will be a good diver. Simply fill a glass with water and
   drop in your packet. *The best packets barely float,*
   with their tops at the water's surface.

2 • After you have found the proper packet, fill an
   empty clear plastic bottle to the top with water.
   (The higher the water level in your bottle, the easier
   this trick is to do.)

3 • Push your unopened condiment packet into the
              bottle, replace the cap,
         and you're done making
         your device!

   4 • To work your device,
      just squeeze the bottle,
      and the packet sinks. Amazing!
      Relax your grip and the saucy diver
      will rise. Miraculous!

The air bubble at the top of the sauce packet determines whether the packet will sink or swim. Squeezing the bottle causes the bubble to shrink. This smaller bubble can't keep the packet afloat, so it sinks. Releasing the bottle makes the bubble expand, which allows the packet to rise.

More to Chew On

The type of device you just made is called a *Cartesian diver.* There are huge Cartesian divers that travel around the world underwater. They are called submarines. Both your device and submarines go up and down in the water for the same reason. You make your condiment go down by squeezing the air in the chamber at the top of the packet. A submarine goes down because water is pumped into an air-filled chamber. In both devices, large and small, a change in density or the way they are packed with "stuff" makes them sink or float.

To find a chapter dense with great activities, turn to "Meat of the Matter," on page 39, and learn a little more about density.

If you like playing with your condiment diver, you should also try "Mealtime Magic," on pages 37–38.

HOLDING CHARGE

Magically stick a straw to the palm of your hand, a window, a door, a wall . . . anywhere.

Plastic straw in paper wrapper
(if no wrapper is available, use a paper napkin)

Tip du Jour: This trick works best when the air is dry (low humidity) and your hands are clean and dry.

1 • Open one end of a new straw. Before removing the wrapper, slide the paper sleeve back and forth quickly. You can do this by firmly grasping the unwrapped end of the straw with one hand and the paper sleeve with the palm of the other hand. If you're using a napkin, wrap it around the straw and slide it back and forth in the same manner. Slide it until the straw and wrapper feel warm (ten to fifteen strokes should do the trick).

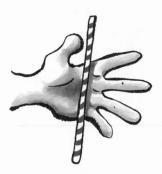

2 • Remove the wrapper and place the straw against the open palm of your hand, which you hold upright.

3 • Slowly move your hand around to show that the straw sticks without glue.

4 • Try this trick again with another straw and place it on another flat but vertical surface (a wall or door, for example). What happens?

8

Did you get a charge out of this trick? You sure did! Or at the very least, your straw did. You electrically charged it! Your superscience superpowers actually moved electrically charged particles. It just so happens that everything is made of atoms, which contain negative- and positive-charged particles. Usually the number of positive and negative charges are equal. When you rub a plastic straw in a paper sleeve, you change, or unbalance, the number of positive or negative charges in your straw. Anytime you bring something that has an unbalanced charge near something that has a balanced charge, they will be attracted to each other. That's what happened between your straw, with an unbalanced charge, and your hand, with a balanced charge. They met and were instantly attracted to each other. Is it love or is it science?

Oh, by the way, if anybody asks, the charge on your straw is about −40 nano coulombs! A *coulomb* is a measure of charge. Just as distance is measured in feet or meters, electrical charge is measured in coulombs.

Do you want more information about electricity? I recommend the highly charged activities in "Cash or Charge," starting on page 56.

SODA POP! STRAW

After you drink your pop, pop your straw!

Lots of plastic straws

Recipe

Tip du Jour: The thick straws you get at fast-food burger restaurants work best.

Getting this trick down right may take some practice. But don't give up if you don't get it right the first time. The pop is worth the effort.

1 • Tightly pinch both ends of a straw.

2 • Twist the straw with a pedaling-type motion.

3 • As you twist, the amount of straw between your fingers should get smaller and smaller.

Twist the straw.

4 • Twist until you can't twist anymore. You should have about an inch (two to three centimeters) of hard, untwisted straw between your fingers.

5 • While you keep holding the straw, have someone flick his or her middle finger at the untwisted portion of straw. They should hit the straw with their fingernail, and they should flick hard! The straw will make a loud pop. If it doesn't pop the first time, flick again or try another straw.

You trapped air in your straw and compressed it. By twisting, you squeezed the air that was in a long straw into the space of a very short straw. The flick compressed the air inside the straw even more, so much so and so fast that the walls of the straw couldn't take it and popped! The untwisted, flicked portion of the straw broke open.

More to Chew On

A lifesaving first-aid action called the Heimlich maneuver works like your straw popper. When food gets stuck in someone's throat, it blocks air from getting into his lungs, but it also traps air in his stomach. A rescuer using the Heimlich maneuver gives the choking person a swift squeeze to his abdomen. The force of the compressed air in the abdomen dislodges the food from the throat.

If you want to have a gas and learn more about gas, check out the activities in "Nice Atmosphere," starting on page 67.

MAIN COURSES

Activities to sink your teeth into

Now that you've tasted an appetizer and whetted your appetite, dig into some more detailed experiments. Each "Main Courses" chapter starts with a brief introduction, which leads to a series of four to seven activities. Some activities even come with a side dish to fill you up more.

Although each chapter and each activity can stand alone, try to go through this book successively. A concept presented in one activity might help you better understand a later activity.

Enjoy!

"I WONDER WHAT I'LL HAVE"

Doing Science

I wonder why. I wonder why. I wonder why I wonder?—Richard Feynman

Well, what will you have? Will it be the tuna surprise or the blue-plate special? What is the blue-plate special anyway? Will you like the tuna surprise?

Science can start the instant you look at a menu, stand in a rain forest, or walk into a high-tech laboratory. All you have to do is wonder. Things to wonder about can be as big and unfathomable as "What is life?" They can also be easy-to-solve questions like "What is the soup of the day?" A sense of wonder is what leads to questions, and questions are what drive science and the investigations that follow.

"Excuse me, I'm wondering what the soup of the day is."
"Our soup today is primordial soup. Would you like a bowl?"
"Is the primordial soup any good?"
"I don't know. No one's ever ordered it."
"What's in it?"
"Amino acids, water, and minerals."
"It sounds good. I'll try a bowl."

The way you try out a possible answer to your question is called an experiment. An experiment can be as simple as ordering a bowl of soup and tasting it; or it can be as complex as launching a spaceship to another planet to see if life exists there. Do you think you'll like the activities and tricks in this chapter? There is only one way to satisfy your curiosity. Experiment and try them!

May I have your order?

I'll have two str
three empty c
an olive, and e
toothpicks

REST ROOM ALIENS

Observation is the key to counting like an alien.

Several pieces of silverware
Two hands

Tip du Jour: Never, ever tell your audience how this game is played. Just do it. They must figure it out on their own. To make the game even more challenging, tell your audience they can't talk to one another. Players can talk only to you, and they can only tell you what they think the answer is. No questions are allowed in this game.

1 • Excuse yourself and go to the rest room. Oh yeah . . . bring this book.

2 • Read the whole activity before returning to your table.

3 • When you return, give a speech (like the one below). Deliver it with feeling!

"The strangest thing happened to me just now. I was captured and held hostage by space aliens in the rest room. I spent years living with them. But because they are so advanced, they were able to warp time. So, compared to human time, I was only gone for a few minutes. The aliens taught me a lot about their culture and ways of communicating. Here, let me show you something I learned. If you want to learn too, just watch everything I do."

Use your imagination! It's okay to make up a different story. Maybe you got sucked down the drain and lived with sewer people, or maybe you had an out-of-body experience while in the lavatory.

4 • The point of this game is for your audience to figure out the special way that aliens communicate numbers. To play, arrange some silverware any

way you like (the more unusual or sillier the pattern, the better). Though your audience's attention will be drawn to the silverware, never mention that they have to look at it. What is important in this game are your fingers (but don't mention *that* either). To communicate a number (from one to ten), hold that number of fingers over the silverware and say how many fingers you are holding out. Your fingers are the true clues, and the silverware is just a way of distracting your audience's attention.

For example, if you want to communicate the number two, hold two fingers out over the silverware and say, "To the aliens, this is a two." If you want to communicate the number seven, rearrange the silverware and hold out seven fingers over this different pattern and say, "To the aliens, this is a seven," and so on.

Say and do the following:

"To the aliens, this is a two."   "To the aliens, this is a seven."

5 • After you present several numbers (and silly silverware patterns), present others, but now ask your audience what number they think you are showing them. Are they able to figure it out? As people catch on, let them take over as the alien game master.

6 • Try many different patterns and numbers. If people still don't get it, try a different silverware arrangement but hold out the same number of fingers. If need be, get rid of the silverware altogether and do it only with your fingers.

7 • After everybody figures it out, ask people what they were thinking as they played.

Did you see that? There, you did it again! You made an observation. You read this book, you smelled the air, and you felt an itch. You constantly observe things.

In the game on the previous page, you made others observe, and you tried to make them observe carefully. They observed you come back from the rest room; they listened to a goofy story; and they watched as you placed silverware in strange patterns. Each time you presented a new number, players gathered more and more information. Hopefully, each player collected enough information to make a guess about what you were doing. Then they tested their guess with even more observations and finally figured out what was going on. It was all in your hands! Or, oh no! Aliens really did abduct you.

Not only does observation help you figure out this game, but it also helps you to figure out how the world around you works, which in turn helps you survive.

Just like everyone else, scientists study the world by observation. They observe something, then ask a question about it.

Believe it or not, everyone who played this game is a scientist. And everyone used a scientific method to figure out what was going on. This scientific method has a very appropriate name too; it's called simply the *Scientific Method*. The Scientific Method is a process that has six basic steps: observing, questioning, researching, hypothesizing, experimenting, and concluding. People playing the game might have done some or all, or repeated several, of these six steps.

Ask the people in your group if anyone did or thought the following:

1 • People made observations. They saw you return from the rest room, heard your story, and saw you place forks, spoons, and knives in weird positions.

2 • They asked themselves a question like: Is this person a nut or what? Should I call the cops? What is this person doing?

3 • They might have *researched* their questions. Research doesn't always mean looking something up in a book. It could be as simple as trying to remember something. Their memory might contain something like: he's never had

hallucinations before; he comes from a normal family; he's been reading that silly restaurant science book. Maybe this has something to do with that book, but I still have no clue as to what's going on.

4 • People might have made a *hypothesis* (a hypothesis is a fancy name for a guess) as to what was going on. They might have thought that maybe the numbers have something to do with the way the pieces of silverware are arranged.

5 • To see if their hypothesis was correct, people might have conducted an *experiment* to test their guess. The experiment was probably as simple as watching the pieces of silverware as you rearranged them.

6 • A few numbers and experiments later, they made a *conclusion*. The silverware has nothing to do with the numbers.

7 • But wait, there's more! If the conclusion is wrong, a new hypothesis must be made, another experiment carried out, and another conclusion drawn. These three steps might need to be repeated over and over until the correct conclusion is made—or until the restaurant closes.

NEW HYPOTHESIS: It's the way he blinks.
EXPERIMENT: Watch his eyes.
CONCLUSION: Nope, that's not it.
Repeat.

NEW HYPOTHESIS: It's his fingers.
EXPERIMENT: Watch his fingers.
CONCLUSION: Yes! It's the way he holds his fingers.

That's it, you got it! You're done!

Did you know that you can now buy insurance for alien abductions?

GRID GAME

Follow some rules, play a game, and learn about science.

Four butter knives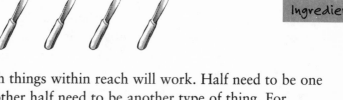

Almost any ten smallish things within reach will work. Half need to be one type of thing, and the other half need to be another type of thing. For example, five ketchup packets and five mustard packets; or five square crackers and five round crackers; or five pink sweetener packets and five blue sweetener packets.

First, lay your four knives down as in the picture below.

Now follow these ten rules.

1 • All rules must be followed.
2 • If a rule is not followed, then players must start a game again.
3 • There may be two—and only two—players.
4 • Each player will use only one type of object. Players must use the same objects throughout the game.
5 • Decide which player will go first. Players must alternate turns.
6 • Players may place one—and only one—object in each of the nine sections formed by the knives.
7 • Only one object may be placed during each turn.
8 • The first player to place three objects in a row—either up and down, across, or diagonally—wins.
9 • If a game is won, the loser gets to make the first move during the next game.
10 • If no player is able to get three objects in a row, the game is considered a tie, and the same player gets to begin the next game.

Begin playing!

19

Most people already know this game. It's tic-tac-toe! Did I need to mention all those rules? You and the person you are playing with probably already know these rules. Rules help people keep score, live life, and have fun. People follow some rules more closely than other rules. If you break a rule in tic-tac-toe, you might make your opponent mad. If you break a rule in baseball, your team might lose. If you break a rule while driving, you could get into an accident. Rules are important in life, and they are also important in science. In fact, some rules in science are so strict that nobody has ever broken them. Don't believe me? Drop something. Really, go ahead. Which way did it go, up or down? It went down, of course. The rules of gravity are always in force; you can't break them. Scientists refer to rules that can't be broken as *laws*. Scientific laws are rules that are impossible to break—like the speed of light, as shown below.

The speed of light is 186,000 miles per second—that's the law.

Scientists figure out the rules of science by observing why and how things do what they do. Engineers, on the other hand, use the rules of science to make stuff. By applying the rules of science, engineers can design and build things like cars, bridges, computers, and ovens.

gAstronomy

Build a model of the solar system out of condiments.

Ketchup-bottle lid
Artificial sweetener
salt and pepper
peppercorns
   (small black balls of pepper found inside a pepper mill)

The sun, the planet Earth (the place where you're eating right now), and eight other planets make up the solar system. All nine planets orbit, or move around, the sun, which is at the center of our solar system. It would be nice if we could put the entire solar system on a table and move the sun and planets around to study it. But because the solar system is so huge, we need to make a shrunken version of it instead. You can get all of your cosmic material right at your table.

1 • Unscrew the top of a bottle of ketchup. This top will represent your shrunken sun.

If the sun is a ketchup top, the planets would be the size of the items listed below. Try to collect these planets and put them on your table.

MERCURY	An extremely small grain of artificial sweetener
VENUS	One small grain of salt
EARTH	One small grain of salt
MARS	One very small grain of artificial sweetener
JUPITER	Medium peppercorn
SATURN	Small peppercorn
URANUS	One piece of coarsely ground pepper
NEPTUNE	One piece of coarsely ground pepper
PLUTO	An almost invisible speck of artificial sweetener

2 • Your shrunken sun and planets can easily fit on your table. Based on each planet's size, do you think you could move each planet into its appropriate orbit? Do you think you could fit the solar system on your table? How big would your table have to be?

3 • If you placed your ketchup top–sun on the edge of your table, you'd have to place the planets according to the list below.

MERCURY	On the other end of a long table (4 feet or 1.3 meters)
VENUS	On the end of the table next to yours (8 feet or 2½ meters)
EARTH	A couple of tables over (11 feet or 3 ½ meters)
MARS	At the other end of the dining room (17 feet or 5 meters)
JUPITER	Somewhere in the parking lot (58 feet or 18 meters)
SATURN	About ⅓ of a football field away (107 feet or 33 meters)
URANUS	About ⅔ of a football field away (215 feet or 65 meters)
NEPTUNE	About a football field away (337 feet or 103 meters)
PLUTO	About a football field and a half away (442 feet or 135 meters)

Food for Thought

What you made is called a *model*. A model in science is an idea, an object, a statement, or a representation that can be used to explain things. One of the neat things about models is that they can be used to explain things that we can't actually see. The better the model, the more it helps to explain something.

If you were able to move every grain of salt and pepper to its appropriate location, then you made a scale model of the solar system. A scale model is one in which all the components of the system or object you're studying are reduced or magnified in equal proportions. In our solar system example, the sizes of the planets and the distances between them are all divided by a common factor of approximately 45 billion. Wow! That's a lot of long division.

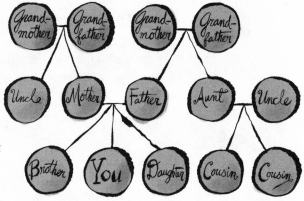

The picture on the previous page is a model of the solar system, but it's not a scale model. In this model, the sizes of the sun and planets are scaled correctly, but the distances between them are incorrect. This model lets you see things easily and on one sheet of paper. It might help you compare planetary features such as the size, color, and orbital rings of each world. But it doesn't tell you anything about the distances between them.

There are many types of models. The one above is an abstract model. Does your mom or dad really look like a circle with words in it? No, I don't think so. Does your brother really have a line coming out of his head? Probably not. The purpose of this model is to show the relationships among family members. It can help you figure out how you are related to different people in your family. You may have heard this type of model referred to as a family tree.

More to Chew On

Let's include our celestial neighbor, Alpha Centauri, in your scale model. Alpha Centauri is approximately 25 trillion miles away. How far away do you think you'd have to put it from your ketchup top–sun so that it fits accurately within your scale model? It may surprise you to know that you would need to put your model Alpha Centauri about 572 miles (921 km) away! Wow—that's like in another state! And remember, your model Earth is just a speck of salt a couple of tables over. It may also surprise you to know that you'd actually need to use three tabletop objects to model Alpha Centauri, since it is a triple-star system and not just a single star. Two of its stars are pretty close to the size of the sun, and the other is quite a bit smaller. So if you have an out-of-state friend who lives about 572 miles away, just send her two ketchup-bottle tops and a pea, and your updated scale model will continue to be fairly accurate.

Alpha Centauri

Ship to:
Anyplace 572 miles away

23

one person

TAKE IT FOR A SPIN!

Figure out which way a bottle top will land even before you spin it. Do this simple "Pop-top" experiment and learn how to win almost every flip (or spin) you toss.

Ingredients

Hard flat table
Twist-off metal bottle cap from a
glass soda-pop, juice, or
ketchup bottle

Recipe

Tip du Jour: The best kind of caps to use are the thin metal ones from wide-mouth tea and juice bottles.

Tails

Heads

1 • Call the top of the lid "heads" and the bottom "tails."

2 • Choose a side. What do you call? "Heads" or "tails"?

3 • Spin the lid on its edge, using a flick from your thumb and forefinger to get it going. Let the lid spin freely. Don't let it bump into anything while it's spinning. Don't let it fall off the table either.

4 • Allow the lid to come to rest. Did you call it correctly?

5 • If you want to know how the top lands almost every time, you need to repeat this experiment several times. Spin the lid some more and record what happens after each spin, as we've done in the table on the following page.

Every time you spin the top, you do an experiment. If you record the outcome of each spin, you are collecting *data*. Data is the information you gather when you do science. Scientists then examine the data, looking for patterns that might help them come to a conclusion.

Do you see a pattern in your data? Did you figure out how to win your spins? If so, you probably noticed that bottle tops don't spin like most coins (half heads-up and half tails-up). Because of their shape, bottle tops almost always land heads-up!

Number of spins	Heads	Tails
1st spin	yes	
2nd spin	yes	
3rd spin	yes	
4th spin		Yes
5th spin	yes	
6th spin	yes	
7th spin	yes	

There will be an interesting activity in your future.

Many people do science to figure out what has happened or what will happen. Making a guess about what will happen is called a *prediction*. Scientists try to predict future events. When will an earthquake happen? When will it rain? When will a comet fly by in outer space? When will dessert arrive?

25

WHAT GOES IN

Making Sense of Senses and Information

Let's say you're hungry. You sit down at a restaurant and look over the menu. A waiter arrives, and you hear him ask, "May I have your order?" A short time later (this is While You're Waiting for the Food to Come), your food arrives. It smells great, and you're ready to start eating. You reach for a fork and hold it in your hand. You scoop up some food, put it in your mouth, and taste it.... Mmmm good, but it needs a little salt.

But food is not the only thing that you put inside your body to help you live. Something else gets into you more often—information. Food usually gets into you only one way: through your mouth. But there are five different types of information that get into you five different ways: visual, through your eyes; auditory, through your ears; tactile sensations, through your skin; smells, through your nose; and tastes, through your tongue.

Like food, you digest information. But instead of being sent to your stomach and intestines, this information goes to your brain, where it is processed. What we know about the world comes from the information we get through our senses. Information not only helps you order your meal but also helps you choose between right and wrong, good and bad, walk and don't walk. Information also affects the way you eat, think, feel, believe, live, and even how you do science.

We see, smell, touch, hear, and taste our way through life. Food may give us the fuel to live, but our senses let us know we are alive.

SEA AND HEAR FOOD

one person

Hear the ocean in a cup of water.

A glass half full of water

1 • Place your ear over the top of a glass of water.
2 • Listen carefully. Can you hear the ocean?

Listen like this.

Don't listen like this.

All water originally comes from the ocean, and most glass is made of melted sand. The water in the glass sounds like the waves at the beach because that's where the ocean meets the sand.

You believe me, don't you? Well, you shouldn't!

Although my silly seashore explanation sounds nice, the noise you hear is actually caused by sounds bouncing around inside your glass. These sounds include noises from people at the next table, cars driving by, and dishes clanking. Be cautious and don't always trust your source of information—not even me. All scientists have to be a little skeptical. "Show me" is not only Missouri's state motto, it is also a rule of thumb for most scientists.

Don't believe everything you're told. Books, TV, and newspapers can be wrong. Even I can be wrong.

On Halloween in 1938, a radio broadcast was heard by millions of people. It was a broadcast of *The War of the Worlds,* a story about the invasion of Earth by Martians. Because the broadcast was made to sound exactly like a real newscast, many people thought this "fake" news story was real. It caused mass hysteria. The public's reaction to this radio show is still studied today to see how false information can affect people.

WELL DONE AND NOT SO WELL DONE

Fool your senses: hot seems cold and cold seems hot.

Ingredients

Three bowls filled with:
    Ice water, water at room temperature, and
        hot water (but not too hot!)
Two plates
Your hands

Recipe

1 • To catch any spills, place the bowl of hot water and the bowl of cold water on a plate. Hide the bowl of room-temperature water.

2 • Have your friend place one hand into the hot water and one hand into the cold water.

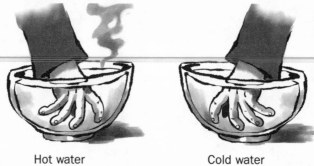

Hot water   Cold water

3 • After about a minute ask her to close her eyes.

4 • Have her lift her hand out of the hot water. Then switch the bowl of hot water with the hidden bowl of room-temperature water and have her put her hand into the new bowl. Ask her, "Is this water hot or cold?" What does she say?

5 • After she answers, do the same thing to her "cold-water hand" and ask her the same question.

The "hot-water hand" should feel cold and the "cold-water hand" should feel hot when each is placed in the room-temperature water. Why? Your skin has tiny sensors called *nerve receptors* that send signals to your brain. Some receptors sense pressure, some sense pain, and others sense temperature (hot and cold).

Your receptors are best at noticing change. When you put a hand in the water, your brain gets information from your temperature receptors that say, "Hey, that's hot," or "Whoa, that's cold." If you keep your hand in the hot water or cold water long enough, your nerve receptors get used to the temperature of the water. The room-temperature water is cooler than the hot water and warmer than the cold water. So when you switch to the room-temperature water, the receptors that got used to the hot water send signals that sense it as cold, and the receptors that got used to the cold water sense the room-temperature water as hot.

Nerve receptors can be tricked easily, especially when it comes to telling the difference between hot and cold. Your body does the best that it can, but unfortunately the information that gets to your brain is not always correct.

What nerve!

Nerve receptors are located all over your skin. One of the nerves' jobs is to help you feel the world around you. Our body and brains are arranged to pay more attention to some parts of our body than other parts.

The picture to the left is a model. (Remember what a model is? See "gAstronomy," pages 21–23.) The body parts of the man below are sized according to how much space our brain allots to signals coming from various parts of our body. Our hands and lips are loaded with nerve receptors; send a lot of signals, or information, to our brains; and are therefore drawn larger. The elbows and knees don't have many nerve receptors and are therefore drawn smaller.

This model is called a Sensory Homunculus.

one person

NOT A WHOLE HAND

**Fool your two eyes and your one brain.
Make a hole appear in your hand.**

Ingredients

Paper place mat

A hand and two eyes

Recipe

1 • Roll your paper place mat into a tube.

2 • Hold the rolled tube with one hand
and place it next to the palm of your
other hand.

3 • Look through the tube with one eye.
Look straight at your palm with the
other eye.

Look here with one eye

...and here with your other eye.

It might take a few seconds, but can you see the hole in your hand? If you
don't see it, try switching the tube to your other hand and look again.

Here's the hole!

One of the main reasons you have two eyes in your head is so that you can see two different images of something. Your left eye and your right eye see and send different visual information to your brain. These different views help you to figure out how big or how far away something is. Your double vision also helps you to see in three dimensions (3-D). Usually, your two eyes send image information that is almost the same. Consequently, your brain has no problem combining the right and left images. However, this trick forces your right and left eyes to see images that are so different that your brain blends them incorrectly. It creates an image of a hole in your hand. Information from our senses goes directly to our brains. But we human beings don't always make correct conclusions from the information that we get. We often make mistakes with information without even knowing it. Sometimes you can't even believe yourself!

We have lots of visual clues that tell us how close or far away something is. Consider for a moment an ice-cream cone heading toward your mouth. As the food comes closer, it looks as if it gets bigger. You can see more of the sides of the food. You change your focus and your eyes turn inward. In figuring things out, your brain not only takes into consideration the visual clues provided by your eyes, but it also interprets how much your eye muscles stretch. Check out the views below.

Food far   Food close

Know when it's time to open your mouth!

31

STOP MAKING CENTS

Everything you see is not all there. Make a coin disappear in midair.

Ingredients

Straw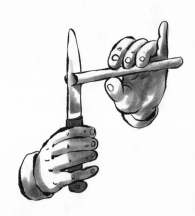
Knife (a plastic knife will work fine)
Coins—one penny, one dime

Recipe

1 • Make a slit at both ends of a straw.

2 • Slide a penny into one of the
slits and a dime into the other.

3 • With coins inserted, hold the straw in the
center with your fingers and at arm's length.

Look here

4 • Close one eye. With the other eye, look
only at your fingers. Although you're
staring only at your fingers, you
should see both coins on the ends of the
straw.

5 • Slowly pull the straw toward your face,
continuing to look only at your fingers.
Does anything happen to one of the
coins?

Food for Thought

Did one of your coins seem to disappear? It disappeared because its image
passed into your eye's *"blind spot."*
Think of your eyeball as a movie screen with an open door in it. Light

32

shines on the back of your eyeball the way a
projector shines light onto a movie screen.
This "eyeball screen" is called the *retina*. But
the information that falls onto your retina has
to leave and travel to your brain. The door it
leaves through is called the *optic nerve*.
Because there are no *visual receptors* located
on this door, or nerve, there is one spot where
you see nothing. It's your "blind spot."

You usually don't notice your "blind
spot" because your brain fills that spot in
with other visual information. Whenever and wherever you look, your brain is
guessing and filling in a part of the picture with information that may or may
not be correct.

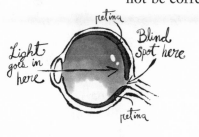

More to Chew On

Have you ever looked up at a starry sky? Have you ever noticed that sometimes
it's easier to catch a glimpse of a faint star if you don't look directly at it? Try
it—it's weird! It turns out that the backs of your eyes are loaded with two different types of receptors: color receptors, called *cones,* and black and white receptors, called *rods*. The area in your eyeball where you get most of your visual
information is crammed full of cones and not many rods. Surrounding this is a
region crammed full of rods and not many cones. Rods are much more sensitive
to faint light than cones and can detect light as feeble as a hundred trillionth of a
watt. Most lightbulbs in your house are
between 25 to 100 watts. By averting your
view just a little, you shift the image of the
star to the more light-sensitive rods. This
helps you catch a peek at a faint star.

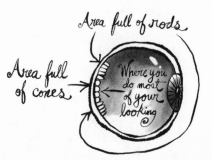

POINTS OF VIEW

Forget your glasses; use a condiment to see. Hey, I've got an even better idea—bring your glasses and still use a condiment to see.

Ingredients

Saltshaker with a metal screw-on top—the smaller the pour holes the better. (Be very careful not to get salt in your eye.)
If you don't have a saltshaker, try a cracker with little holes in it. (Ritz crackers seem to work best.)
Menu or something to read

Recipe

Tips du Jour: Don't forget to put the saltshaker top back on tightly.
Try this experiment with a friend's prescription glasses.

Most people have one "goodish" eye and one "baddish" eye (that is, one eye sees better than the other). You will need your "baddish" eyeball for this experiment. If you are lucky and both your eyes see equally well, borrow someone else's glasses and put them on. This should help worsen your sight. This can also really dramatize the effect for those with good and bad eyes.

1 • Close your "goodish" eye and try to read a menu with your "baddish" eye. How does it look?

2 • Remove the top from a shaker of salt. Tap the metal top on a table to get rid of any salt in it.

3 • Hold the shaker top to your "baddish" eye and close your "goodish" eye. Hold the top so that the holes are about an inch or two in front of your eye. Do the same if you are using a cracker.

Hold the shaker top in front of your eye.

Hold the shaker top in front of a pair of borrowed glasses.

34

Do the same if you're
using a cracker.

4 • Look at your menu through the small holes.
Does it make a difference?
Is it clearer or did it make it blurrier?
How does it look?

Food for Thought

When the metal top is screwed on a saltshaker, the small holes control the flow of
salt that pours out. When held up to your eyes, these little holes control the way
light information gets into your eye. Usually, light travels through structures in the
front part of our eyes called the *cornea* and the *lens*. These structures try to
arrange light so that you see things clearly. If the shape of your lens or cornea is
not just right, what you see will be distorted (if it's distorted enough, you might
need glasses). When you place a small pinhole (or set of pinholes) in front of your
eye, it takes over the job of arranging light so that your cornea and lens don't
have to. For most people, pinholes, especially small pinholes, arrange light better
than their own naked eyeballs, so they see things more clearly.

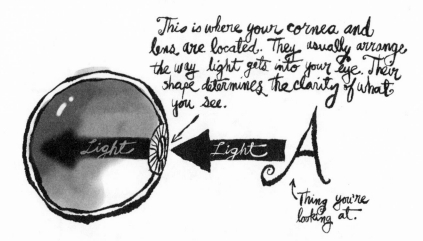

This is where your cornea and lens are located. They usually arrange the way light gets into your eye. Their shape determines the clarity of what you see.

Light

Light

Thing you're looking at.

Viewing the letter *A* through your naked eye.

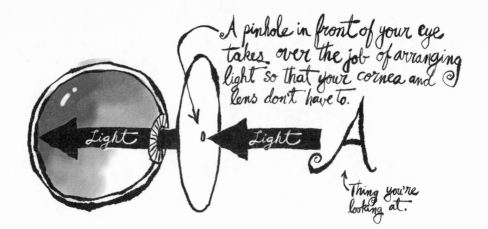

A pinhole in front of your eye takes over the job of arranging light so that your cornea and lens don't have to.

Light

Light

A

Thing you're looking at.

Viewing the letter *A* through a small hole.

Vision is very important to us because it's the primary way we take in information about the world. Even though we have four other senses, 70 percent of our body's sense receptors are clustered in our eyes.

Don't forget your glasses.

MEALTIME MAGIC

Show your supernatural powers by sinking a condiment.

Ingredients

The "Condiment Diver" in the "Appetizers" section is great for doing magic tricks. Set up a bottle with a condiment diver in it, as described on pages 6–7.

Recipe

1 • Find someone or a group that hasn't seen a condiment diver yet.

2 • Hold the entire device with one hand and point at the packet inside the bottle with your other hand.

3 • Say to your audience, "I will now make the sauce packet sink with my thoughts."

4 • Do the following:

Repeat the words *Sink, sink, sink.* . . .
Gently and secretly squeeze the bottle with one hand.
Slowly move the pointing finger of your other hand downward as the packet sinks.

Even though the packet is sealed inside the bottle, it will look as if your finger is magically tugging it down.

5 • To raise the diver, say the words *Rise, rise, rise.* Slowly release your squeeze, and draw your finger upward.

Food for Thought

Is it magic? Well, if you limit the amount of information you have given your audience, it sure looks like magic. Think about it. How many times do magicians let you see how a trick works? Do most magicians let others poke around their equipment? Do they tell you how it's done? No, I don't think so!

After you perform a magic trick, follow these three rules.

1 • Don't tell anyone how it's done.
2 • Don't let anyone touch your equipment.
3 • Don't repeat a trick too many times.

If you follow these rules, you can be a magician and keep what you're doing a mystery. However, by using the scientific method (see "Rest Room Aliens," pages 15–18), a scientist like you can figure out almost any magic trick.

Giving misinformation also helps when doing magic.

MEAT OF THE MATTER

Things That Matter: Volume, Mass, Density, and Center of Gravity

This can be a heavy subject, so you might want to prepare yourself. Before reading this chapter, why don't you order the biggest meal on the menu. While you're at it, why don't you order a dessert or two. Begin eating and start reading.

Everything you eat, taste, breathe, hold, or see is made of something. That something is called *matter*. It's the stuff of the universe. While you're thinking about this matter thing, why don't you finish scooping your meal into your mouth . . . I'll wait. . . . Good, now wipe your chin. Oh, and get rid of that thing stuck between your teeth.

Did you finish the meal you ordered? If you did, your body now has more *mass*. Mass is the amount of matter something has, and after you put a large meal down your throat, your body definitely contains more matter.

Do you think you're more attractive after having a lot to eat? Maybe you don't, but the Earth definitely does. In fact, it finds you so attractive that it can't help but gravitate toward you. You see, one of the weird things about things with mass—and all things have mass—is that they get drawn toward one another. That attraction is called *gravity*. The more mass something has, the more it is pulled toward other objects. The Earth happens to be the biggest, most massive thing around you. Consequently, you, as a much smaller lump of matter than the Earth, are currently being pulled toward it. The more matter you contain, the more you are pulled toward the Earth.

So, now that you're more firmly planted on Earth, maybe you can stomach doing some activities about matter.

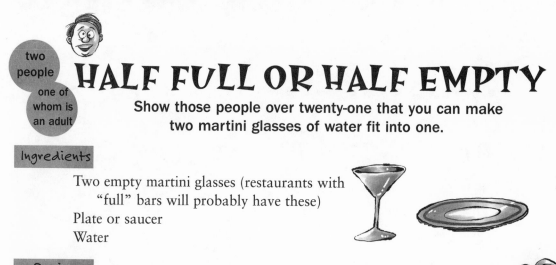

HALF FULL OR HALF EMPTY

Show those people over twenty-one that you can make two martini glasses of water fit into one.

Ingredients

Two empty martini glasses (restaurants with "full" bars will probably have these)
Plate or saucer
Water

Recipe

Tip du Jour: Ask an adult to help you with this experiment.

1 • Borrow two empty martini glasses and a pitcher of water.

2 • Pour water into both glasses. Fill them both to exactly the same height, about half an inch below the rim. Call one glass no. 1 and one glass no. 2. (If you have enough time, and no one is watching, an optional method would be to fill one glass completely to the top with water, then pour exactly half of this glass's contents into the other, empty glass.)

3 • Make sure everyone sees that the water level in both glasses is the same. Hold up glass no. 1 and ask, "Is this glass half full or half empty?" Most people will say the glass is more than half full.

Fill each gla about this fu with water.

4 • Place glass no. 1 on top of a plate or saucer to catch any drips.

5 • Pick up glass no. 2. Carefully and slowly pour it into the glass on the plate. Keep pouring even if a small bulge of water forms above the rim of glass no. 1. (This water bulge actually has a name. It's called a *meniscus*.)

Meniscus

6 • Remarkably, you should be able to empty the entire contents of one glass into the other without spilling any.

(If the water does spill, you poured too much water into the two glasses at the beginning. Try your experiment again, but this time use the optional method in Step 2.)

The glass that looked more than half full was really more than half empty.

Everything is made of something called matter, and all matter takes up space. That means it takes up room in three dimensions: front to back, side to side and up and down. You might often hear these dimensions referred to as *length,* *width,* and *height,* and the space they define as *volume.*

Closets, boxes, and parking garages are things that can hold matter. So are martini glasses, which are designed to hold liquid matter. They are upside-down cones and are much wider at the top than at the bottom. Because of this shape, the lower portion of the glass does not hold nearly as much liquid as the upper portion of the glass. When you include the "side to side" and "front to back" dimensions, the top of the glass is large enough to handle the extra liquid from glass no. 2.

These are large

side to back to side

front to side

top to bottom

Even though this is small

Have you ever wondered how much liquid there is in most drinks? If your drink was in a can, bottle, or juice box, you can find out the volume of the liquid inside by looking at the label.

A typical can of soda holds a volume of 355 milliliters (or 12 fluid ounces). To think of this volume another way, you could fit 355 small cubes that are 1 centimeter long by 1 centimeter wide by 1 centimeter thick (1cm × 1cm × 1cm) into the can.

You can fit 355 of these cubes into a typical can of soda.

Wowee!

ADDING ICE

Does your cup runneth over?
Are you really getting all the drink that you think?
Discover how much of your soda pop is liquid and how much is ice.

Large disposable cup filled with both soda pop and
   ice
Large empty disposable cup (same size as filled cup)

Recipe

Do you like soda pop or do you like ice? If you like soda pop but you put a lot of
ice in your cup, you might not be getting as much soda pop as you think.

1 • Fill a large disposable cup. Put in as much ice and soda pop as you
   normally would. Look inside your cup and see how full it is.

2 • Hurry to a table and get ready to do your
   experiment. Don't wait too long, because
   you don't want your ice to melt.

3 • Tip the full cup over an empty cup. Let the
   soda pop dribble into the empty cup, but
   don't let any ice fall into the empty cup.

4 • When you are done pouring, look at
   how much soda pop is in one cup and how
   much ice is in the other.

Pour the soda pop, not the
ice, into the empty cup.

Food for Thought

Surprise! Depending on how much ice you use, you might be getting a lot less
drink than you think. Two pieces of matter (and both soda pop and ice are
matter) can't take up the same space at the same time. This means that where

there's ice there can't be soda pop. If you use less ice in your cup, it might take a little bit longer for your drink to get nice and cold, but you'll have more soda pop to drink.

More to Chew On

Now that your one drink has been separated into ice and soda pop, try this: pour your ice into the cup with the soda pop. Watch what happens to the level of the soda pop. Does it go up or down?

It went up, of course! The ice, which is a solid, *displaced,* or pushed aside, the soda pop, which is a liquid. The ice took up so much room in the cup that the soda pop had no place to go but up. The height that the soda pop rose by is related to the volume of the ice.

One of the first people to understand the relationship between solids, liquids, and displacement was a Greek fellow by the name of Archimedes. He didn't figure this stuff out by wearing a white lab coat or by putting ice into soda pop. The story goes that he discovered it while he was taking a bath. As Archimedes was getting into a tub 2,200 years ago, he noticed that the water level rose. When he realized what was happening, he ran down the streets naked, yelling, "Eureka—I found it!" Archimedes' observation led to his fundamental realization regarding *buoyancy* (why things float or sink). This is so important to science that it was named after him; it's called *Archimedes' Principle.*

one
person

IN THE DRINK

Find out which soda makes the best float, diet or regular.

Ingredients

One unopened can of regular soda pop
One unopened can of diet soda pop (same brand
and flavor as the regular soda pop)
Two clear pitchers, each containing no ice and filled
about halfway with water

Recipe

1 • When you order your drinks, ask the waiter or waitress not to open the cans. Oh yeah, make sure to tell him/her that you're really thirsty and would like a pitcher of water too. No, make that two pitchers of water, thank you very much.

2 • Place one can in one pitcher and the other can in the second pitcher. That's it. Look where the cans go. Do they float or do they sink?

Food for Thought

Everything being Equal™, the diet drink floats and the regular (sugared) drink sinks. Are you surprised? Well, consider this: both cans are the same size (their volume is 12 fluid ounces or 355 millileters) and are filled with the same amount of artificially flavored liquid. However, they do not contain the same amount of matter. From our experiment, we see that one can is slightly heavier. How can this be? Read the ingredients label on each can and find out!

When you read the ingredient list, you discover that one of your sodas has sugar and the other has a sugar substitute called aspartame. Pure aspartame is hundreds of times sweeter than sugar. So you don't need as much aspartame as you do sugar to make something sweet. By weight, there is a lot more sugar in the regular drink than aspartame in the diet drink. If you add up the amount of weight of

44

the aluminum can, the liquid, and the air at the top of the can, the regular drink weighs more.

Density is a term used to refer to how concentrated matter is in an object. To figure out an object's density, you compare its mass (the amount of matter something has) with its volume. If something has a high density, it means the object has lots of matter crammed into a given space. If something has a low density, it means the object has only a little bit of matter crammed into a given space. Okay, you say, but why does one can float and the other sink?

Let's say you were able to make a column of water the exact size and shape as the two cans of soda pop. The aluminum can of regular soda pop (which also contains a pocket of trapped air under the lid) would weigh more than the column of water, and the aluminum can of diet soda pop (which also contains a pocket of trapped air under the lid) would weigh less than the column of water. This means that the can of regular soda is denser than water, and the can of diet soda is less dense. Anything that is denser than water sinks, and anything that is less dense than water floats.

More to Chew On

Vessels like the naval ship below are made of steel. Steel is much denser than water. So why does it float?

If you add the mass of the steel and the mass of the air in the hollow spaces inside of the ship, overall it would contain less matter than an equally sized volume of water—that's density for you!

Thousands of tons of steel and it still floats!

MUSCLING IN ON DENSITY

Concentrate on matter by experimenting with food on your table.

Bread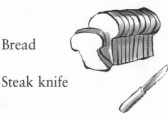

Steak (or pork chop)

Steak knife

A couple of glasses of water

Tips du Jour:

- *Don't go to a really high-class restaurant, because the piece of beef that you order needs to have a decent amount of fat on it. A trimmed piece of meat just won't work in this experiment.*
- *Some of these steps might appear gross to people at other tables, not to mention to people at your own table, so be sure to check with your parents first, and try to be discreet (make it a secret).*

1 • Order a big thick steak or prime rib. While you're waiting for your food to come, see if you can get an order of bread and a couple of glasses of water without ice.

2 • When the bread and water arrive, tear off a chunk of bread and remove the crust.

3 • Tear off a second piece of bread about the same size and also remove the crust. Smash this second piece of bread into the smallest ball you can.

4 • Place the smashed bread and the regular, unsmashed bread into a glass of water. Watch what happens. Does either piece of bread sink or float?

5 • Time for the main course. When your steak arrives, cut out two small pieces of beef that are the same size—one, a small piece of lean meat and the other, a small piece of solid fat.

6 • Plop your two pieces of beef into a glass of water and watch what happens.

Assuming your bread and cow were normal, the regular piece of bread and the blob of fat floated, and the smashed piece of bread and the piece of meat sank. Why do you suppose that happened? Well, bread and meat are made of matter, and for that matter, so is water. Things sink or float depending on how concentrated their matter is compared to the concentration of matter in water. In other words, if something is denser than water, it sinks; if it is less dense, it floats (remember the soda can from "In the Drink," the previous activity).

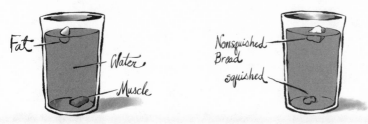

Matter can be packed together differently in different things. A fluffy piece of bread is not too dense, so it floats. (However, after a while, the bread may have absorbed water and sunk.) A smashed piece of bread obviously has a higher concentration of matter. Because of its increased density, smashed bread sinks.

Meat is muscle, and fat is, well, fat. There is more matter concentrated in muscle than in fat. This is harder to see than a smashed and unsmashed piece of bread. However, you can see the effect of differences in meat density, which causes the muscle to sink and the fat to float.

This experiment actually came about because of a conversation I had with Don Lawrence, an NFL football coach. He asked me how putting a player in a dunk tank helps to determine a player's percentage of body fat.

Many doctors and athletic trainers use tubs of water with chairs suspended in them to evaluate body composition. These chairs are attached to scales. To use the device, a patient or an athelete is put in the chair and lowered into the water. The weight of someone underwater indicates how much body fat he has. The more fat someone has, the more he floats and the less he weighs underwater.

DENSITY DRIPS

Make liquids drip up and down.
Create a homemade (or restaurant-made) lava lamp.

Ingredients

Tall, clear glass of cold water, no ice
Salad oil (olive or sesame oil is best)
Salt

Recipe

Shake in salt

1 • Fill a glass about three-quarters full with cold water.

2 • Slowly pour some oil into the glass. Because oil is less dense than water, the oil will float. Stop pouring when you have a layer of oil about ½ inch or 1 cm thick on the water's surface.

3 • Next, sprinkle salt generously on top of the oil and watch what happens.

4 • Add more salt or any other condiment to see what else might happen.

Food for Thought

Oil is less dense than water, so it floats. Salt is more dense than both water and oil, so it sinks. What makes things interesting in this trick is that the oil tends to cling to the salt temporarily. Together, the oil and salt blobs are denser than water, so they descend to the bottom of the glass. As the blobs go down, the oil coats the salt and keeps it from dissolving. After sinking, the oil soon yanks free from the salt and floats up again.

Salt can be found in many places. But would you expect to find a huge lump of salt rising up through the ground? Formations known as *salt domes* exist in various locations around the world. Salt domes can be miles wide, and they form when salt rises up from deep underground. Salt that was buried tens of millions of years ago in flat layers collects into huge columns that migrate to the surface of the earth. It takes millions of years for these formations to migrate upward through layer after layer of rock. The salt rises because the surrounding rock is denser and presses on the salt with tremendous force. Under the right conditions, salt can flow like a liquid—a very, very slow-moving liquid. If the salt finds a weak point in the rock above, it will work its way up and into it.

If you look around your table, you might find a bottle of Tabasco sauce. This hot sauce is made of hot peppers, salt, and vinegar and is manufactured in Avery Island, Louisiana. Avery Island is a salt dome and is also home to the oldest salt mine in the United States.

A SALT AND GRAVITY

**Balance a saltshaker on its edge and discover
that the center of gravity is the key to being up-standing.**

Ingredients

Salt

Hard, level tabletop

A standard saltshaker with a square- or
  hexagon-shaped base (round won't work;
  a shaker that is half full tends to work better than a full shaker)

Recipe

*Tip du Jour: Your table must remain perfectly still during this demonstration.
Keep all arms and legs clear of the table; hold all applause, and perhaps your
breath, until it's done!*

1 • Sprinkle a pinch of salt on top of a table and form a
     small pile.

2 • Place the saltshaker so that one edge is resting in
     the pile.

3 • Slowly lean the shaker to one side and find the angle
     at which it just begins to fall.

4 • Tilt the shaker slowly in small increments and gently
     rock it back and forth until it is balanced. Let go of
     the shaker when it feels like it can stand on its own.
     It will take patience, practice, and time to get the shaker
                       to balance, but it will be
                       worth it. Trust me!

Gently rock the
saltshaker back
and forth until it
balances.

5 • Once the shaker is balanced, gently blow
     as much of the salt away as you can.

Blow the salt away.

50

Have you ever heard the term *freestanding*? It doesn't mean that something normally has to pay in order to stand. It means that something can stand on its own without being bolted, glued, welded, or tied down. Your saltshaker is freestanding.

All objects, including the saltshaker, have a special point either inside or outside of their bodies called the *center of gravity* (you can also call it the center of mass). The center of gravity of an object is based on its mass and how the mass is distributed throughout the object. The center of gravity of the saltshaker is located somewhere inside the bottle, above its base.

If you took your pepper shaker (which happens to be a nonleaning, freestanding, center-of-gravity-over-the-base condiment dispenser), you could slide it toward the edge of a table. Don't do this, but if your pepper shaker was slid far enough, it would fall as soon as the shaker's center of gravity was no longer over the table. So long as the center of gravity of a freestanding object is supported from directly below, it won't fall.

Center of gravity of the shaker (still over the table)

Look at the bottom of your leaning saltshaker. You'll probably notice at least one small grain of salt wedged next to the shaker. This small box-shaped crystal is helping the shaker stand up by letting it lean against it. You won't be able to see this, but somewhere directly above the salt crystal and shaker's bottom edge is the shaker's center of gravity. As long as the shaker's center of gravity is over a base of support, even a small one like the salt grain and shaker's edge, it will stay up. Knocking or moving the table may cause the shaker's center of gravity to fall out of alignment with its base of support. When this happens, the shaker falls over.

If the center of gravity of the shaker is moved over the edge of the table, it will fall.

The center of gravity must be above
the salt crystal and the shaker's edge.

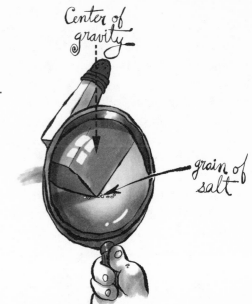

Center of gravity

grain of salt

More to Chew On

One of the most famous buildings in the world is having trouble with its center of gravity. The tall, round building below is the Leaning Tower of Pisa. This popular tourist attraction is known for its tilt. Luckily, the center of gravity of this structure is still located over its base of support. If the tower's center of gravity moves over too far, it's bye-bye building.

The center of gravity of
this tower is still over
its base of support.

FORKS AND CORKS

**Simply the most elegant and fascinating demonstration
you can do at a restaurant.
Make a cork and two forks seem to float in air.**

two
people

one of
whom is
an adult

Two forks (metal silverware)   A toothpick

A match

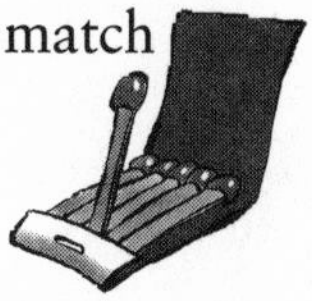

A water glass
or wineglass

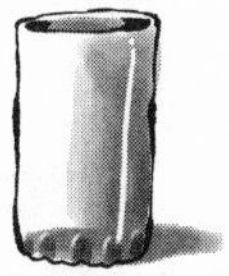

A cork

Tips du Jour:

- *Use extreme caution, as you'll be working with pointed objects and matches. Get adult supervision when doing this trick.*
- *Check all assembly pictures carefully.*

1 • Push a fork into the side of a cork as shown at right, but be very careful. The fork should be inserted toward the bottom of one end of the cork.

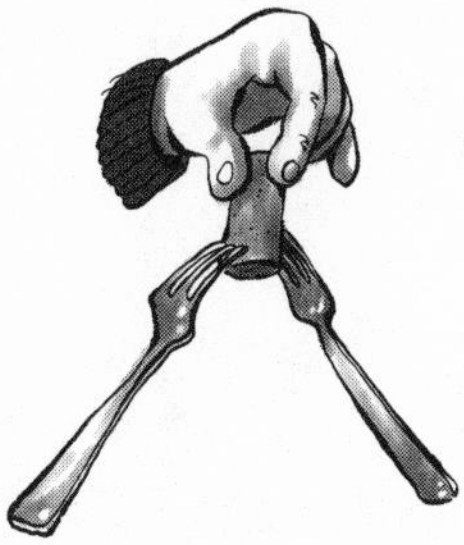

2 • Push another fork into the cork from the opposite side so that the forks form a mirror image of each other. Notice in the picture how both forks are positioned. (Different styles of forks might require slightly different angles—try it and see if you need to make adjustments later.)

3 • Hold the cork as shown. Now you need to locate the spot where the toothpick will be inserted. On the end where the forks are located, find the edge of the cork (where the end and side of the cork meet). On this edge (or rim), locate the point directly in the middle between the forks. Carefully insert a toothpick at this location. Angle the toothpick upward quite a bit (maybe 30 to 45 degrees). Push the toothpick in just far enough so that it will be able to support the weight of your device.

4 • Next comes the hard part, but you can do it. Hold the fork-and-cork device and rest the upwardly angled toothpick on the rim of a glass as shown. Now gently and slowly slide the device back and forth until it feels like it balances, and let go! Don't give up too easily. If it doesn't balance after a couple of tries, rebuild your device. But this time, change the angles of your toothpick and forks. You might need to try a couple of different variations, but eventually you'll get it.

5 • Once the device is balanced, the portion of toothpick located on the inside of the rim isn't needed to support it and can be removed. A really dramatic way of doing this is by burning it. Get an adult to supervise this part. Have the adult light a match and ignite the portion of toothpick inside the glass.

6 • The toothpick will almost always stop burning when it reaches the glass rim. Blowing the red, glowing ember adds to your dramatic presentation and helps to remove ash from the end of the toothpick.

7 • Sit back and behold!

Food for Thought

Isn't this activity the coolest? I mean the hottest?!

It all has to do with center of gravity (remember this concept from "A Salt and Gravity," pages 50–52?). But before explaining what's going on with this device, let's take an imaginary trip to a playground and talk about your center of gravity.

Your center of gravity is an invisible spot located inside your body. It is the place where you balance right and left, front and back, and top and bottom. To find your center of gravity, you could lie or stand on a seesaw, just as in the pictures on the next page. If you moved your body so that the seesaw didn't

Center of gravity

Center of gravity

teeter, you could locate your center of gravity. It would be directly above the wedge or fulcrum of the seesaw, probably near your belly button.

The device that is balancing on the rim of your glass doesn't have a belly button, but it does have a center of gravity. If you look at your device, you should notice that the fork handles, the heaviest part of your contraption, are situated below the burnt toothpick. Because of this, the center of gravity of your device is actually located directly below the charred end of the toothpick. It's weird, but the place where it balances, right and left, front and back, and top and bottom, is floating in midair.

Location of the center of gravity.

Remember from "A Salt and Gravity" that in order for you to stand and not fall over, you must have a base of support directly below your center of gravity. Well, the reverse is true for hanging objects, or things that are supported from above; the center of gravity of an object must be directly below a support. Your fork-and-cork device is a hanging object and the rim of the glass where the charred end of the toothpick rests is the support. Your device will remain suspended on the rim of the glass as long as its center of gravity is located directly below the charred end of the toothpick.

CASH OR CHARGE

An Electrically Shocking Account of Attraction and Repulsion

Have you ever taken a bite from an apple? If you have, then you've bitten off, chewed, swallowed, and digested matter. The matter in your apple is made of incredibly tiny particles called *atoms*. Atoms are so small that if you were somehow able to enlarge a small apple to the size of the Earth, then the atoms in the apple would be approximately the size of the original apple.

Everything is made up of atoms, and every atom is made up of even smaller parts. Atoms are composed of three fundamental particles: *protons, neutrons,* and *electrons.* Protons and neutrons are held deep in the heart of atoms, and electrons whiz around them. These tiny particles carry an electrical charge. Electrons are negatively charged (–); protons are positively charged (+); and neutrons have no overall charge.

Most of the matter you find hanging around contains the same number of electrons and protons. This means the positively charged particles cancel out the negatively charged particles, and what you have is electrically neutral matter. If you happen to find some matter that has more electrons than protons, then that piece of matter has an overall negative charge. If you find some matter that has more protons than electrons, then that piece of matter has an overall positive charge.

Interesting things can happen right at your table when you investigate charge. Hopefully the activities in this chapter will have a positively electrifying effect on you.

CUP O' CHARGE

Be impulsive and be repulsive. Move a cup with what's on your mind—your hair!

Ingredients

Two empty and dry Styrofoam cups
A head of clean, dry hair
Four to six straws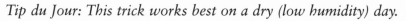

Recipe

Tip du Jour: This trick works best on a dry (low humidity) day.

1 • Lay down four to six straws on a flat hard tabletop. Position the straws about a finger's width apart.

2 • Rub the two empty Styrofoam cups on your hair at the same time. Rub them several times back and forth. You'll know when you're ready to go to the next step because when you lift the cups away from your hair, your hair will seem to stick to the cups.

3 • After rubbing, immediately place both cups, bottoms up, on top of the straws. Place them about a thumb's width apart, and try to position the cups so that the sides you just rubbed on your head are facing each other.

4 • Let go of the cups and see what happens.

5 • Did the cups move away from each other? Try it again and see if it happens again.

The sides of the cups that you rubbed against your hair should be facing each other.

Where each cup was rubbed against your hair

When you let go, your cups should have moved apart. Even if you push them together again, they'll spring back.

Even if you use a good shampoo, when you rub the cups on your head, your hair and the cups become electrically unbalanced (don't worry, it doesn't hurt your hair). Usually, the atoms in your hair and the atoms in the Styrofoam cups contain about the same number of electrons as protons (negatives and positives). By rubbing the cups on your head, things get ripped apart and rearranged. It turns out that after rubbing the cups there are more electrons than protons left on the cups and more protons than electrons left on your head (that's positive thinking for you!). When the negatively charged particles get placed on the cup, they stay put. Things that don't move are called static. So what you created was *static electricity,* and now your cups are both negatively charged. When you brought both cups together, they actually moved apart, or repelled each other, right? That's what same charges do—they repel. Negative charges repel negative charges. If both cups had received a positive charge instead, they would have done the same thing—they would have repelled too. One rule for charge is: *Same charges repel.*

Try the side dish below and learn about another rule for charges.

SIDE DISH

Be More Attractive

Tip du Jour: You might need another hand (literally) to do this extended version of the last trick. Ask a friend to help.

1 • Rub the two cups on your hair as you did before.

2 • Place the cups on the straws, but this time, space them several thumb's widths apart. Don't let go yet.

3 • Have someone else place one hand between the cups.

4 • Now let go. Which way did the cups go? They should have moved toward your hand.

5 • Try it again, but this time move your hand in and out from between the cups. See if you can create a rhythm and rock the cups back and forth.

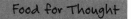
The rule about same charges repelling could be called a rule of thumb, fingers, and hands. You have about the same number of protons as electrons in your hand. You can't feel this, but when you put your hand between the negatively charged cups, the negative charges in your hand are repelled. Many of the negatively charged particles in your hand move as far away from the cups as they can. Since you now have fewer negatives in the part of your hand that is in between the cups, that part of your hand is now more positive (the technical term for this is *induced charge*).

He's out of here—
Come on over!

Are you ready for another rule? *Opposite charges attract.* Since your hand was overall positively charged and the cups were overall negatively charged, they move toward your hand.

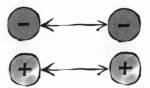

Same charges repel.

Opposite charges attract.

One of our country's first scientists made the choice of which electrical charge would be called "plus" and which "minus." His name was Benjamin Franklin.

CAN CAN

Truly one of the most mystical demonstrations you can do anywhere. Make a soda pop can follow your command without touching or blowing it.

Ingredients

One empty and dry aluminum can
One empty and dry Styrofoam cup
Clean head of hair
Flat surface

Recipe

Tips du Jour:

- *It's important to have an empty, dry can.*
- *This trick works best when the air is very dry (low humidity).*
- *It's best if you have a clean and dry head of hair.*
- *If no Styrofoam cup is available, it is possible to get this trick to work with a charged straw (see "Holding Charge," on pages 8–9).*

1 • Place your can on its side on a long flat table or on the floor.

2 • Rub the Styrofoam cup against your hair as you did in the previous experiment, "Cup O' Charge." This makes an area of static electricity on the cup.

3 • Hold the charged part of the cup (the side that you rubbed against your head) near the side of the can. Unbelievably, the can will start to roll toward the cup.

4 • Draw the cup slowly away from the can while keeping the can close enough for it to "feel" the tug of the cup. This will allow the can to continue rolling toward the cup.

Direction in which cup should be moved

Direction of roll

5 • To reverse direction, hold the cup on the opposite side of the can. To make the can go faster, hold the cup closer to the can, or rub the cup on your head again to increase the static charge.

Food for Thought

The can has hordes of negatively charged electrons rushing all around its metallic body. The cup, on the other hand, after you rubbed it on your head, has an area of concentrated, nonmoving—or static—electrons. When the cup is brought near to the can, electrons on the part of the can closest to the cup are repelled and "run" to the other side of the can (remember: same charges repel).

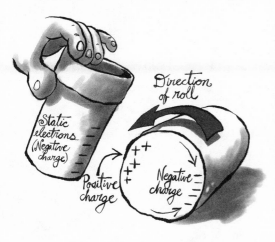

Direction of roll

Static electrons (Negative charge)

Positive charge

Negative charge

After the electrons have fled, positively charged protons are left behind. This area of the can is now overall positively charged. Since opposites attract, the can is pulled toward the cup. As the can rolls, the electrons keep "running" to the opposite side to get away from the cup, but the positive protons are always left behind to get pulled toward the cup.

More to Chew On

Have you ever gotten dressed up and gone to a really nice restaurant? Have you ever touched a doorknob at said restaurant and gotten zapped? Lots of fancy restaurants have expensive wool carpets. Wool is the hair of sheep. When you drag your shoes across this hairy carpet, you get charged. As you reach for something like a metal door-knob, you induce an opposite charge in it (just like the cup and can). When your finger gets close enough, ZAP! Charges leap off, and you get shocked.

61

BENDING WATER

Bend water. This is an amazing trick—you gotta do it!

Three Styrofoam cups
Toothpick

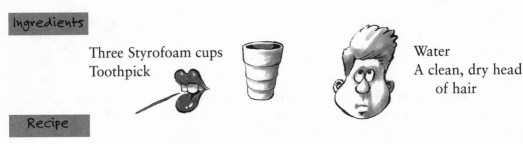

Water
A clean, dry head
of hair

Tips du Jour:
- *This trick works best when the air is very dry (low humidity).*
- *It's best if you have a clean and dry head of hair.*
- *If no Styrofoam cups are available, you can use paper cups to drip and catch some water. You can substitute a charged straw for the cup that you rub on your hair. (See "Holding Charge," on pages 8–9.)*

1 • First you need to make a device that will drip a steady, narrow stream of water. To make the device, just push a toothpick into the bottom of a Styrofoam cup, but leave the toothpick in the hole in the base of the cup.

2 • Fill the cup with some water, but don't remove the toothpick yet. When it's left in, the toothpick plugs the hole that it made, and the cup won't leak. You now have your dripper.

3 • Take another empty Styrofoam cup and rub it on your hair. This rub gives the cup an electric charge, so rub it good.

4 • Now you'll need some help. Have someone place the third empty cup on a table and have him or her hold the "dripper" directly above it. Pull the toothpick plug on the "dripper" and allow the water to flow into the empty cup below.

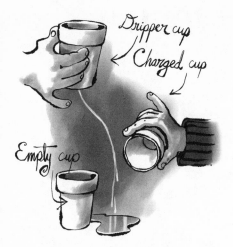

Dripper cup

Charged cup

Empty cup

5 • Now hold the charged cup near the stream of water. Make sure the part of the cup that was rubbed on your head is closest to the running water. You'll be amazed by what happens next.

6 • The stream of water bends toward the charged cup! Try not to get too much water on the charged cup, and make sure the water doesn't sprinkle all over your clothes.

Food for Thought

Water is made up of atoms. The smallest piece of water that you can call water is composed of three atoms. One type of these atoms is called oxygen, and the other two are identical atoms called hydrogen. When a substance needs more than one atom to be that substance, the grouping that the atoms form is called a *molecule*. Water is a molecule, and the shorthand way of writing the formula for a water molecule is H_2O.

This is a molecule of water. An oxygen atom is Mickey's head, and two hydrogen atoms are Mickey's ears.

The atoms of water just happen to prefer to arrange themselves in the pattern at the left. If you look hard enough, you can see why water's nickname is "the Mickey Mouse molecule."

Atoms are made up of electrons (negatively charged), protons (positively charged), and neutrons (no charge). The way electrons are distributed throughout a water molecule makes the oxygen atom more negatively charged and the hydrogen atoms more positively charged. (There are more electrons by Mickey's mouth and fewer electrons by Mickey's ears.)

When water flows out of the bottom of the cup, the molecules tumble any way they want: face first, ear over ear, head over head, etc.

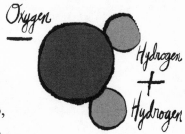

Oxygen

Hydrogen + Hydrogen

63

Remember the past few activities, where you rubbed a cup against your head? The cup receives a negative charge from your hair. As those tumbling, carefree water molecules come nearer and nearer to the negative charge of the rubbed cup, the molecules rotate. The mouse's head (oxygen) turns so that it is pointed away from the charged cup. Mickey's head is negative, and the charged cup is also negative. (Remember: same charges repel.) Since the head is pointed away from the charged cup, this means that the ears are pointed toward the cup. The ears, which are hydrogen and positively charged, are attracted to the cup; opposites attract.

Since each falling water molecule's positive end is pointed toward and attracted to the charged cup, the water gets drawn in that direction. Gravity keeps the water falling downward while the charged cup keeps tugging the water sideways. This is what causes the unbelievable bend in the flow.

Water molecules rotate

Curved path of water

Original path of water

More to Chew On

Bending water is a great party trick that everyone can see. But water's oddly charged nature allows it to do many other things. For example, it can dissolve salt. Like water, table salt is also a molecule. Salt is composed of equal numbers of sodium atoms and chlorine atoms. Also like water, salt has an uneven charge distribution. Sodium has a positive charge and chlorine has a negative charge. When water comes near salt, the negative side of water is attracted to the positive part of a salt molecule, and the positive side of water is attracted to the negative side of a salt molecule. Water uses the "muscle" in its charge to pry apart the sodium and chlorine atoms and dissolve salt.

Sodium atom

Chlorine atom

One molecule of salt

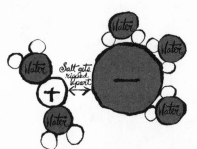

Water
Water
Salt gets ripped apart
Water
Water

Water's positive and negative nature helps pull salt apart.

WRIGGLE WRAPPER

Can you make a straw wrapper wriggle and grow?
An electrifying trick everyone should know.

Straw in paper wrapper
Glass of water

1 • Bunch up your wrapper while it is still on the straw by sliding both ends of the wrapper together.

2 • Slide the bunched-up wrapper off the straw and onto the table.

3 • To make your wrapper grow, dip the tip of one end of your straw into a glass of water. Then place your finger over the other end of the straw. This will trap some water in the tip of the straw.

4 • Place the end of the straw with the trapped water directly over the wrapper. When you remove your finger, a little bit of water should drip out and onto the wrapper. Watch what happens!

Drip some water onto the wrapper.

Did you see the wrapper wriggle and grow? Did you also notice that as the water soaked into the paper, it slowly absorbed and worked its way along the length of the wrapper? But why does water do this? Remember from "Bending Water," pages 62–64, that water is known as "the Mickey Mouse molecule." Part of the molecule has a positive charge, and the opposite side has a negative charge. The charged nature of water allows it to cling and soak into things. When the small drop of water touched the crumpled wrapper, the water crept from dry paper fiber to dry paper fiber. As each fiber absorbs water, it swells and straightens out. This makes the wrapper get longer and grow.

More to Chew On

This ability of water to creep along because of its charge is called *capillary action*. Capillary action makes it possible to soak up spills with napkins, paper towels, and sponges. The faster the capillary action, the quicker a mess can be cleaned up.

NICE ATMOSPHERE

Having a Gas with Air

Have you ever sucked up a drink through a straw? I'll bet that you haven't. No one has ever actually done that. When you get liquid into your mouth through a straw, your mouth does not pull up the liquid; the air above your head pushes it up. You see, we live at the bottom of an ocean of air. This ocean is called the *atmosphere*. The atmosphere not only extends out to the horizon in every direction, but it also goes straight up into the sky for miles and miles. If you could weigh the atmosphere, it would weigh over 5,000 trillion tons! All this air not only allows us to breathe and live; it also surrounds us and pushes against us. In fact, the square to the right, 14.7 pounds of air equivalent of a 6.7 kg push is called *air pressure*. molecules bashing and even as you read, has about pressing against it (or the mass resting on it). This It's caused by zillions of gas bumping into things.

When you drink through a straw, what you really do is place your mouth over the straw and decrease the pressure inside the straw. Since the air pressure, or downward push, on the drink outside of the straw is greater than the downward push on the inside of the straw, the liquid rises and goes into your mouth . . . ahh, pure liquid refreshment.

So why don't you finish your drink, take a deep breath, and begin investigating air pressure by turning this page.

Lower air pressure inside of the mouth

Higher air pressure on the surface of the drink.

Lower air pressure inside of the straw

TIPSY

Turn an open bottle upside down for a draining experience—or maybe not.

Ingredients

Water
Empty glass bottle (any kind will work)
Paper napkin or any small piece of paper

Recipe

Tip du Jour: Do not use a carbonated beverage like soda pop for this trick.

Fill water to the top.

1 • After you finish emptying a glass bottle, refill it to the brim with water. Fill it so high that you get a little water bulging at the top of the bottle.

2 • Tear off or find a piece of paper that is a little bigger than the mouth of the bottle.

3 • Place the paper over the mouth of the bottle.

4 • Lightly tap the paper on top of the bottle to make sure it gets wet and makes a good seal with the bottle's glass lip.

Tap the top of the piece of paper

5 • Although this is a cool trick and may whet your appetite to learn more about air pressure, you don't want it to end up cool, wet, and on your lap. As a precaution, follow the additional extremely important *Tips du Jour* at the top of page 69.

Tips du Jour:
- *When you flip your bottle, do it over a bowl, plate, or pitcher.*
- *Do not touch the paper on the lip of the bottle at any time while it's tipped.*
- *Do not shake the bottle while tipped. All movements should be slow and steady.*

6 • It is now time to turn your bottle upside down . . . slow and steady. If your trick works, no water will spill out. If not . . . remember that part about cool and wet and on your lap?

Food for Thought

The answer to how this trick works is all around you—really! It's the air! Air pushes on everything you see: the floor, the walls, the ceiling, and the paper on the mouth of the bottle. This pushing that air does is called air pressure. Even though gravity is yanking the water inside the bottle down, the upward push of air pressure outside the bottle is greater than the downward pressure inside the bottle.

More to Chew On

Air pressure is so strong that you can flip a filled bottle that is over three stories tall and water still wouldn't spill out.

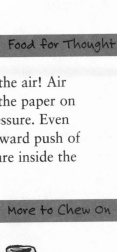

33-foot tall bottle

Although the water in the bottle pushes down, air pressure pushes up.

Air pressure

69

ATOMIZER

Spray a fine mist by using two straws, a glass of liquid, and a good set of lungs.

Two straws   Glass of water

I suggest starting with a glass of water and two straws. If you work your way up to stickier, smellier, or more colorful liquids such as cola or juice, be careful where you aim.

1 • Hold one straw vertically in a glass of water with one hand. Don't let the end of the straw touch the bottom of the glass of water (this might block the flow of water).

2 • With your other hand, hold a second straw horizontally. One tip of the horizontal straw should be inserted into your mouth, and the other end should be held adjacent to the tip of the vertical straw to form a 90-degree angle.

3 • Now blow, and blow hard!

4 • If your straws are set up properly, your blowing should raise the liquid up the vertical straw. When the liquid reaches the top, it spews out in the direction of your blow.

Tip du Jour: If the water doesn't spew forth, try the following:
- *Check the angle of your straws and try to keep them steady as you blow.*
- *Make sure the vertical straw is not touching the bottom of the cup.*
- *Shorten the distance the liquid has to go up the vertical straw. You can do this three ways:*
    - *a. Hold the vertical straw farther down into the cup.*
    - *b. Raise the level of liquid in the cup by adding more liquid.*
    - *c. Reduce the length of the vertical straw. You can do this by cutting off part of the straw with a knife.*

Check the angle of your straws.

Imagine you're at a baseball game and the ninth inning just ended. You're at the hot dog vendor, and you want to join your friends, who are across the main corridor at a souvenir stand. But thousands of people are walking in front of you. You want to reach the other side, so you step into the flow of people. After getting carried along with the crowd, you end up in the parking lot. Well, a similar thing is happening where the two straws meet, only it's a molecular rerouting.

As the airflow yanks molecules out of the vertical straw, air pressure goes down inside that straw.

Atmospheric pressure pushes down on liquid and forces it up this straw.

When you blow though the horizontal straw, you cause billions of air molecules to flow over the top of the vertical straw. If any air molecules are near the top of the vertical straw, they get swept into the horizontally rushing flow. As the molecules from the vertical straw get yanked out and carried away, the air pressure inside the straw goes down. If you remember from the introduction to this chapter, if the pressure inside of the straw goes down, the air pressure outside of the straw pushes liquid up the straw. When the liquid rises high enough in the straw, it meets the rapidly moving horizontal air and gets carried along with it, causing the spray.

Devices that use this technique to dispense liquids are called *atomizers*. Some of the coolest art is created with atomizers. These types of atomizers are known as air-brushes. Airbrushes use rapidly flowing air to draw up and shoot out paint. Instead of blowing with his or her mouth, an artist typically uses a mechanical pump that produces a continuous stream of air. The whole contraption can be held in the hand!

Other common devices use this method as an efficient way to dispense misted liquids. Antique perfume bottles are atomizers. They use rubber bulbs to pump and propel the air and smelly stuff. Carburetors use this technique to produce a fine mist of gasoline that is injected into an engine's piston chambers. This atomized mist is easily ignited by an electric spark and sends your car cruising down the road.

one person

UNCANNY MOTION

Stump yourself and others with the motion of these cans.

Ingredients

Two empty soda pop cans
A hard flat surface, like a table

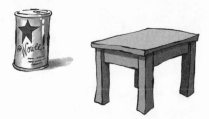

Recipe

1 • Lay two empty soda pop cans on their sides about a thumb's width apart on a flat tabletop.

2 • If you blow straight down and between your cans, in which direction will the cans move? Make a hypothesis first, and then blow as shown to the left and find out!

3 • Here's another question. In which direction will the cans move if you blow between them from the side? Make another hypothesis, and then blow between them from the side as shown in the picture to the right above.

Food for Thought

When you blew down between the cans, did the hypothesis in your noggin match what you saw? I'll wager that the cans did exactly what you thought they'd do. They rolled apart, didn't they? When you blow down, the air hits the table and then hits the cans. This air moves the cans apart.

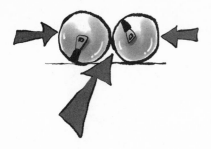

How did your hypothesis fare when you blew between the cans from the side? Most folks probably guessed that the cans would move apart again. Did they? Nope. The explanation for this one is definitely a little weirder. When you blow from the side, you allow the air on the outside of the cans to push the cans in.

What you've just demonstrated is a fact that airplane designers use all the time—air that has been speeded up has a lower pressure. This means that the air that you blew between the cans has a weaker push on the cans than the air on the outside of the cans. Since the air on either side of the cans has higher pressure and, consequently, more push, the cans roll toward each other.

More to Chew On

Have you ever seen an airplane wing? The top has more of a curve than the bottom. As an airplane moves through the air, the air has to speed up to make it up and over the top of the wing. Since air is forced to travel faster over the top surface of the wing, the air pressure is lower there. One of the things that helps planes fly is "lift," which results from the pressure difference between the top (lower pressure) and bottom (higher pressure) of the wing.

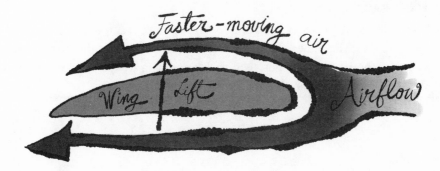

SIDE DISH

Try this variation on the can experiment and guess what will happen.

Two straws

Recipe

1 • Lay two straws down on the table, then place two cans on their sides on top of them about a thumb's width apart.

2 • Blow straight down, just like in the first experiment, and watch what happens!

More Food for Thought

Are you surprised by what happened? The cans rolled together! Because you used the straws, the air exits and passes underneath the cans instead of hitting them. Since the flow of air between the cans has a lower pressure than the air on either side of the cans, they roll together.

BAG-BLOWING BATTLE

**See who can blow up a submarine-sandwich bag faster.
Will the winner be someone who read this book or
someone who didn't?**

Two long and narrow plastic submarine-sandwich bags

*Warning du Jour: Always use extreme caution anytime a plastic bag is near your
face.*

1 • Before competing in any bag-blowing competition, first read this activity
all the way through.

2 • Find a sucker who will compete against you. (Remember, when it comes
to air pressure, there is no such thing as a sucker.)

3 • Have your bag-blowing foe stand so that he or she can't see what you are
about to do. (For example, you could stand back to back).

4 • See if you can find someone who will say, "Ready, Set, Go!"

5 • As that person is saying "Ready, Set, Go!," move the bag away from your
face. Hold the opening of the bag about ten inches (25 cm) away from
your mouth and open the bag with your fingers. Take a deep breath and
blow.

6 • Your bag will totally fill with one blow. As soon as it does, close the end
of your bag.

You should do this.

Don't do this.

7 • Your opponent will probably still be puffing away when you yell, "Finished!"

8 • You're now ready for the Bag-Blowing Olympics.

Did you cheat?! More air than just what came out of your lungs went into the bag. By holding the bag away from your mouth, you blew a stream of air through "still" air and into the bag. (No air is ever really still—air molecules are moving all the time.) As you remember from "Uncanny Motion," pages 72–74, speeded-up air causes lower air pressure. So as the air traveled from your mouth to the bag, the higher-pressure air surrounding the stream of air got mixed in and carried along for the ride and into the bag. Since more air went into the bag, it filled faster, and you won!

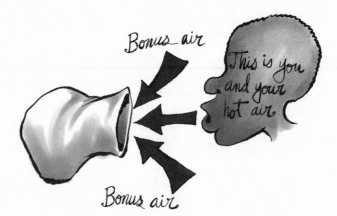

Bonus air

This is you and your hot air

Bonus air

DESSERTS

Topping off your meal

Check, Please

. . . .

ENDNOTE

Are you full yet?
Did you enjoy your dining experience?
Did this book make it to at least a couple of restaurants?
Is it covered with food stains?
I hope so!

I also hope it entertained you, helped you entertain others, and gave you an appreciation of science. If you haven't yet shared a scientific adventure with anyone, do them a favor: the next time you go out to eat and see someone sitting at a table, sipping from a straw, and just staring blankly out a window, walk over to them and say, "Excuse me, would you like to know what else you can do with that straw?"

May you never be bored while dining again!

—Eric

P.S. When you're not eating or waiting for your food to come, check out my Web site at *www.doscience.com*.

After-Dinner Mints

● ● ● ● ● ● ● ● ● ● ● ● ● ● ● ● ●

ACKNOWLEDGMENTS

Kay Lawrence—thanks for being so great; Ronnee Yashon— thanks for believing in this book and me; Paul Doherty (the smartest guy in the world) and everyone at the Exploratorium and the Wright Center for Innovation in Science Education—thanks for all your help and support; and all my friends who put up with me during dinner—thanks.

The San Francisco Dining Bureau:
Brian ("Density Drips") and Donna Swarthout, Chris ("Soda Pop! Straw") Witt, the Moxleys, the Wagstaffs, the Russells, Modesto Tamez, Linda Shore, Karen Kalumuck, Lori Lamertson, Coral Clark, the Talkoffs, and Mary Petrofsky.

The Boston Dining Bureau:
Elisa Berrol, Kelly McCarty, Britt Hammond, the Robinson family, Eric Chaisson, Ellie B., Robert L., Dana Berry, and Jules Yashon.

The Upstate New York Dining Bureau:
The Lawrence family.

The Los Angeles Dining Bureau:
The Muller family, especially my mom.

Jenny Dunham and Sarah Caguiat—thanks for taking a chance on this book; The Resource Area for Teachers—thanks for letting me be testy with your teachers.

Thanks to all the waiters, waitresses, and buspeople who brought me an extra straw, glass of water, or napkin.

Digesting Your Food

● ● ● ● ● ● ● ● ● ● ● ● ● ● ●

GLOSSARY

Air pressure: the force exerted by the atmosphere on the surface of an object

Archimedes' Principle: a scientific rule, named after Archimedes, a Greek mathematician and inventor, that explains why things sink or float when immersed in a fluid

Atomizer: a device that shoots a fine spray or mist

Atoms: tiny particles that make up all matter

Blind spot: an area at the back of your eye that has no visual receptors to receive information about what you see. You don't see this area as a blank spot because your brain fills it in with other visual information.

Capillary action: the ability of a liquid to creep along a solid (for example, a napkin fiber). This is due to molecular and electrical attraction.

Cartesian diver: an object that can be made to sink or float by changing the size of a bubble of trapped air. (This, in turn, changes the object's density.)

Center of gravity: a special point inside or outside an object where the object is balanced left to right, front to back, and top to bottom

Conclusion: a decision made regarding the outcome of an experiment

Cones: visual receptors in the eye that sense light in color

Cornea: a structure of the eye that, along with the lens, focuses light entering it

Coulomb: a unit of electrical charge

Data: information you gather when you do science

Density: a measurement that compares an object's mass to its volume; density determines how concentrated matter is in an object.

Displacement: the moving or pushing aside of one material by another

Electron: one of three tiny particles that make up an atom. Electrons have a negative electrical charge.

Experiment: a test designed to see whether a hypothesis (or theory) is correct

Gravity: a force in nature that draws objects to one another. Gravity is what draws your body to the Earth.

Hypothesis: a guess about the answer to a problem or question

Induced charge: the movement or unbalancing of electrical charge in one body caused by another

Laws: rules in science that cannot be broken

Lens: a device that focuses light; in eyes, lenses are located just behind the cornea.

Mass: the amount of matter inside something

Matter: the stuff that makes up everything

Meniscus: the curved surface at the top of a column of liquid

Model: an idea, object, statement, or representation that can be used to explain things

Molecule: the smallest grouping of atoms that forms a substance. (For example, two hydrogen atoms and one oxygen atom form a molecule of water.)

Nerve receptors: tiny sensors in your body that send signals about the world to your brain

Neutron: one of three tiny particles that make up an atom. Neutrons have no overall electrical charge.

Optic nerve: the path through which visual information travels from your eye to your brain

Prediction: a guess about what you think will happen

Proton: one of three tiny particles that make up an atom. Protons have a positive electrical charge.

Researching: the process of consulting different sources (books and articles, other people, your memory, etc.) for information

Retina: a layer at the back of your eye that contains receptors sensitive to light

Rods: visual receptors in your eye that sense light in black and white only

Scientific Method: a process used to discover answers to questions

Static electricity: electrical charge caused by stationary, or unmoving, electrons

Visual receptors: tiny sensors in your body that send signals to your brain with information about what you see

Volume: a measurement that indicates the amount of space something takes up

Leaving a Tip

● ● ● ● ● ● ● ● ● ● ● ● ● ● ●

RESOURCES AND REFERENCES

Bodanis, David. *The Secret Family: Twenty-four Hours Inside the Mysterious World of Our Minds and Bodies*. New York, N.Y.: Simon and Schuster, 1997.

Bosak, Susan V. *Science Is . . . .* Ontario, Canada: Scholastic Canada Ltd., 1991. (A source of fascinating facts, projects, and activities)

Cassidy, John, Paul Doherty and Pat Murphy. *Zap Science*. Palo Alto, Calif.: Klutz Press, 1997. (Also includes "Condiment Diver," page 42)

Feynman, Richard Phillips, *Six Easy Pieces: Essentials of Physics Explained by Its Most Brilliant Teacher*. Reading, Mass.: Addison-Wesley Publishing Co., 1996.

Hewitt, Paul. *Conceptual Physics*. Reading, Mass.: Addison-Wesley Publishing Co., 1992.

Liem, Tik L. *Invitations to Science Inquiry*. Chino Hills, Calif.: Science Inquiry Enterprises, 1990.

Murphy, Pat, Ellen Klages and Linda Shore. *The Science Explorer Out and About: Fantastic Science Experiments Your Family Can Do Anywhere!* New York, N.Y.: Henry Holt, 1997. (Also includes "Density Drips" under the title "Salt Volcano," page 104)

The Physics Teacher Magazine. Published monthly by the American Association of Physics Teachers, College Park, Md. Check out Martin Gardner's "Trick of the Month" column. (Also includes the first publication of "Condiment Diver" (May 1996), "Holding Charge" under the title "Static Sticky Straw" (November 1995), and a letter to the editor by Michael Brown, from the physics department at Miami University, in which he determined the field strength on a statically charged straw (January 1996).

Suzuki, David, and Barbara Hehner. *Looking at the Body*. New York, N.Y.: John Wiley and Sons, 1991.

———. *Looking at the Senses*. New York, N.Y.: John Wiley and Sons, 1991.

Compiled by UNESCO. *700 Science Experiments for Everyone*. New York, N.Y.: Doubleday, 1962.